Frank Junior Hurtado Talavera

IMPACT OF EVALUATION ON CURRICULUM PLANNING

Frank Junior Hurtado Talavera

IMPACT OF EVALUATION ON CURRICULUM PLANNING

IN THE EDUCATIONAL CONTEXT

ScienciaScripts

Imprint
Any brand names and product names mentioned in this book are subject to trademark, brand or patent protection and are trademarks or registered trademarks of their respective holders. The use of brand names, product names, common names, trade names, product descriptions etc. even without a particular marking in this work is in no way to be construed to mean that such names may be regarded as unrestricted in respect of trademark and brand protection legislation and could thus be used by anyone.

Cover image: www.ingimage.com

This book is a translation from the original published under ISBN 978-620-0-40427-5.

Publisher:
Sciencia Scripts
is a trademark of
International Book Market Service Ltd., member of OmniScriptum Publishing Group
17 Meldrum Street, Beau Bassin 71504, Mauritius
Printed at: see last page
ISBN: 978-620-0-99707-4

IMPACT OF EVALUATION ON CURRICULUM PLANNING IN THE EDUCATIONAL CONTEXT

SUMMARY

The purpose of this research is to reveal the importance of assessment in curricular planning among teachers in an educational unit in the city of Quito, Ecuador. Its argumentative value is based on the need to emphasize the adequate use of evaluation techniques and instruments in curricular planning as the basis for a quality educational process, based on the ministerial guidelines of the Ecuadorian Agreement MINEDUC-201600020A. Methodologically, it is based on the phenomenological-hermeneutical method, with a qualitative approach and a non-experimental design. The type of research is field-based and descriptive, with an educational unit in the city of Quito, Ecuador, as the study site, and three (03) teachers attached to the institution as key informants. The information was obtained through direct observation techniques and the interview with its respective semi-structured script instrument. The analysis and interpretation of the information is done through two epistemic filters based on Leal (2005), and validated through the triangulation of sources. The findings led to the following final reflections: teachers recognize curricular planning as an organized structure of the contents to be dealt with in the educational process; the curricular planning they carry out is based on the contents to be developed according to the students' weaknesses and strengths; and the assessment techniques they most implement in their pedagogical practice are work tables, presentations and examinations.

Keywords: Curriculum Planning, Educational Praxis, Assessment Techniques and Instruments

ABSTRACT

The purpose of this research is to reveal the importance of evaluation in curriculum planning among teachers in a educational unit in the city of Quito, Ecuador. Its argumentative value lies in the need to emphasize the proper use of evaluation techniques and instruments in curricular planning as the basis of a quality educational process, based on the ministerial guidelines of the Ecuadorian MINEDUC-201600020A Agreement. Methodologically it is located in the phenomenological-hermeneutical method, with a qualitative approach and a non-experimental design. The type of research is field and descriptive, having as a scenario of study an Educational Unit in the city of Quito Ecuador, and as key informants three (03) teachers attached to the institution. The obtaining of information was used through direct observation techniques and the interview with its respective semi-structured script instrument. The analysis and interpretation of the information is carried out through two epistemic filters supported by Leal (2005), and validated through the triangulation of sources. The findings led to the following final reflections: teachers recognize curricular planning as an organized structure of the contents to be treated in the educational process; the curricular planning they carry out is based on the contents to be developed according to the weaknesses and strengths of the students; and the evaluation techniques that are most implemented in its pedagogical practice are the work tables, exhibitions and exams.

Keywords: Curriculum Planning, Educational Praxis, Evaluation Techniques and Instruments.

INDEX

INTRODUCTION

The investigation was conducted in an Educational Unit in the city of Quito - Ecuador, attending from high school to the unified general high school, which we will call Educational Unit from now on, the name of the institution will not be mentioned due to the request of the authorities of the same. As of the 2016-2017 school year, the Educational Unit is implementing the changes established in the Ministerial Agreement MINEDUC-201600020A issued by the Ministry of Education of Ecuador in relation to its curriculum, which has had a direct impact on teachers, As they adhere to and comply with the new ministerial guidelines, they develop short, medium and long-term plans in which their pedagogical practice can be effective and efficient. However, the determination of strategies to carry out the educational process becomes cumbersome as they have to reflect the appropriate evaluation techniques and instruments.

It should be noted that evaluation is the determining factor in obtaining results from the academic point of view, only through it can the student's cognitive development be measured, and with it his or her abilities and skills. However, the teacher is responsible for the student's academic development, since it is he who, through curricular planning, teaches the didactic units established according to time, making use of techniques that promote metacognitive competencies focused on the teaching-learning process, through instruments with structured knowledge that stimulate and allow evidence to be obtained about their cognitive and behavioral processing.

Based on the above, a qualitative research was carried out in order to respond to the following specific purposes: a) Diagnose the knowledge about curriculum planning in the teachers of the Educational Unit in Quito, Ecuador; b) Identify how the curriculum planning process is developed in the teachers of the Educational Unit in Quito, Ecuador; and c) Analyze the techniques and evaluation instruments that are developed in the curriculum planning of the teachers of the Educational Unit in Quito, Ecuador. For them, the following theoretical approach was made:

THE EVALUATION

Since the fifth century BC, great Greek philosophers such as Socrates were already applying questionnaires as part of the evaluation process of their practices, but it was in the nineteenth century when the basis for an evaluation model emerged with the birth of the traditional school. On the other hand, by 1845 in the United States, studies were carried out in Boston schools to measure student performance through an evaluation test applied by Man. Later, in 1898, in the midst of industrialization, a researcher by the name of Rice carried out spelling tests on more than 30,000 students for eleven years, concluding that progress in education was minimal.

According to Rosales (1990), in the last decades in the field of evaluation several researchers have focused on the study of the following dimensions:

a) The use of teaching objectives as a reference for evaluation (R. Tyler, 1949, 1975).

b) The extension of the scope of evaluation beyond the previously determined objectives (M. Scriven, 1967).

c) The impact on the need to evaluate processes rather than outcomes (M. Scriven, 1967; D. Stufflebeam, 1971; M. Parlett, and D. Hamilton, 1972; S. Kemmis, 1986).

d) Evaluation as a collection of information to inform rational decision-making. The need for clarity and timeliness of information (L. Cronbach, 1963; M, Parlett and D. Hamilton,

1972; R. E. Stake, 1975; S. Kemmis, 1986; D. L. Stufflebeam, 1971)

e) The use of a pluralistic and predominantly naturalistic methodology in the collection of information (B. MacDonald, 1971; M. Parlett and D. Hamilton, 1972; E. Eisner, 1985).

f) The interest of considering, within the scope of evaluation, the context in which teaching takes place, the impact on its characteristics (M. Parlett and D. Hamilton, 1972; E. Eisner, 1985).

g) Consideration of evaluation not as a simple collection of data, but as a task of judging from the data, on the characteristics of teaching. The need to determine criteria that serve as reference points (R.E. Stake, 1975; *Joint Committee on Standards for Educational Evaluation,* 1981; M. Scriven, 1976)

h) The need to proceed with the development of a meta-evaluation, with the implicit task of identifying criteria for evaluating the evaluation (*Joint Committee on Standards for Educational Evaluation,* 1981; S. Kemmis, 1986). (p. 21).

On the basis of the above, it is necessary to stress that the study dimensions of these researchers cannot be considered alien to each other, as the characteristics complement each other. Therefore, R. Tyler is related to assessment according to objectives, emphasizing the learning process and the curriculum; M. Scriven to formative assessment, taking into account the needs of those involved in teaching; L. Cronbach to assessment based on data search for decision making, maintaining a balance in the methodology of experimental and natural procedures; R. Stake and M. Scriven to assessment with a judgement function, M. Parlett and D. Hamilton with a holistic and contextual evaluation, E. Eisner with an artistic evaluation, S. Kemmis and the *Joint Committee* with the meta-evaluation, corresponding to the evaluation of the evaluation responding to the principles of rationality, autonomy and responsibility, community of interests, plurality of value perspectives, plurality of evaluation criteria, opportunity in the elaboration and distribution of information, and adaptation.

There are various definitions of evaluation that can be obtained, since it is seen as an independent field of study, the product of educational and methodological currents and interpretations. It is important to emphasize that evaluation is closely related to the quality of the educational level, since it is through evaluation that student performance is measured in an institution and its methodology to be applied is governed by the government entities of a country. In addition, it verifies the performance of the teacher with respect to the educational process where the fulfillment of the objectives is reflected.

Of course, each student has his or her own pace of learning and it is the teacher who, through his or her curriculum planning, will make use of the necessary strategies to develop the cognitive and behavioural processes in each of them, measured by means of techniques and assessment instruments in accordance with the content.

In addition, these authors emphasize Quiñonez (2003), when expressing: "evaluation is a component of the teaching-learning process, it is part of the dynamic that from the beginning of each teaching activity is determined by the objective-content-method relationship, it is not a complement or an isolated element" (s/p). In this sense, the above-mentioned triad should be integrated into the assessment process applied by the teacher in order to guarantee the purposes of the teaching-learning process. (See *Figure 1*).

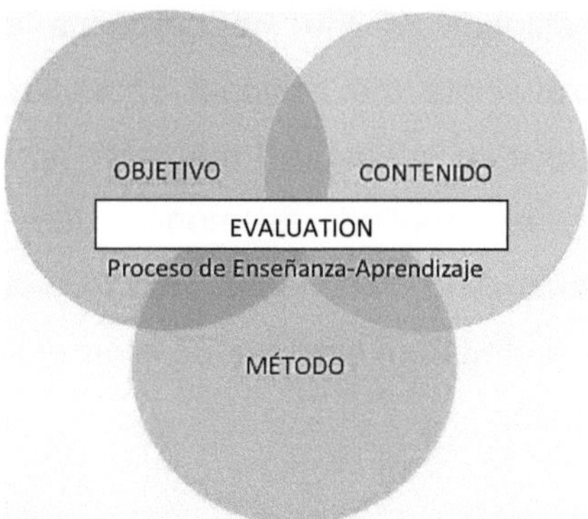

Figure 1. Evaluation Triad.
Note: Source: Own elaboration. (2019).

In *Figure 1*. Triad of the Evaluation, we can see the aspects that favour the teaching-learning educational process, in which the objectives, the contents to be taught and the method in which it is applied to the students are intertwined, and these are determining factors in their success or failure. Likewise, Navarro and col. (2017), quote Velásquez de Díaz (2011), emphasizing that the evaluation of learning is considered a permanent process of information and reflection on the production of learning that requires for its execution a diagnosis where the needs of the student are determined and the objectives are directed, explaining and evaluating the performance of the student to measure the capacities, weaknesses, strengths, and promoting participation in the educational process. In this sense, the student must be informed about the evaluation of the learning in which he or she participates.

In Ecuador, the National Institute for Educational Evaluation (INEVAL) is responsible for developing and strengthening constitutional rights in the field of education, which comes into force in accordance with article 67 of the Organic Law on Intercultural Education and article 346 of the Constitution of the Republic. Its objectives are to comprehensively evaluate the National Education System and its components, to develop studies on the most appropriate research methodologies to be applied, to monitor the instruments and procedures for conducting evaluations, and to process and analyse the information collected from evaluations in order to construct quality indicators in education.

ASSESSMENT TECHNIQUES AND TOOLS

During the evaluation process, it is very important to vary the use of techniques and instruments to promote better academic performance in students, as part of the educational process. In various countries such as Mexico, the National Open University, Research and Graduate Office (2002), has conducted studies on evaluation, with the result that the use of various techniques and instruments by teachers encourage the fulfillment of educational work in the classroom, making the teacher aware of the learning status of the student.

In turn, the evaluation techniques are known by Vazquez (2011), as: "a set of mechanisms, means, resources, procedures, ways that serve to collect, preserve, organize, analyze and quantify all the information in the research conducted" (p. 33). Therefore, they are proposals of the evaluation process that will depend on the curricular planning elaborated by the teacher, since it is where these are reflected according to the didactic units and the time of execution. Similarly, Parra (2013), establishes that: "this is determined according to the type of information that is required to be collected, with the purpose that one wishes to fulfill in the evaluation, and with the moment or phase of the process in which one intends to have an impact" (p. 22). In addition, these techniques are accompanied by evaluation instruments as a resource which are intended for specific purposes, therefore, the technique depends on the instrument.

Likewise, for this author, the assessment instrument is known as: "the specific development of a structure for testing knowledge, performance or competence, related to knowledge or a set of knowledge, skills or applications" (p. 22). In summary, the instrument is the tool that allows an evaluation process to be developed, and the way in which it is applied is due to the technique, therefore, they correspond. Figure 2 below shows the above-mentioned relationship.

Evaluation techniques and instruments

Techniques	Instruments
Objective knowledge test	Written test Oral Examination Objective review
Remark	Records Checklists Scales
Interviews	Question Script Portfolio
Survey	Questionnaire

Figure 2. Note: Source: Own elaboration. (2019).

Some evaluation techniques can be visualized with their corresponding instrument or information collection structure, as well as for example observation, which is used when there is an intention directed at the knowledge object, obtaining information in a systematic, valid and reliable way corresponding to a scientific intention, or when it is freely investigated without pre-established criteria giving rise to an open observation. We speak of closed observation when it is delimited by instruments. In this technique the instrument where the observations are recorded can be the register, the checklist or a scale.

It is essential to strengthen the correct use of evaluation techniques and instruments in the development of curricular planning in the teaching-learning process, since the educational quality of institutions depends on it.

CURRICULUM PLANNING

Educational institutions have the obligation to comply with the curriculum as the project that determines the objectives of school management based on epistemological, pedagogical, psychological, ideological and anthropological foundations. As Bolaños and Molina (1990) point out, citing Hainaut (1980): "a curriculum is an educational project that defines: a) the ends, goals, and objectives of an educational action; b) the forms, means, and instruments for assessing the extent to which the action has produced fruit" (p. 24). This means that the curriculum is centered between the two-line conception as teaching that emphasizes content and the teacher; and learning that prioritizes the experiences obtained and the student through planning.

Along the same lines, Roger Kaufman (1973), in his systemic model, notes that curricular planning is concerned only with determining what should be done, so that later practical decisions may be made for its implementation. Planning is a process for determining "where to go" and for establishing the requirements for reaching that point in the most efficient and effective manner possible.

In addition, curriculum planning is the plan that explicitly guides the teaching and learning process within a given educational institution, since it allows for the construction of knowledge, establishing requirements in an effective and efficient manner. Therefore, it is necessary to emphasize that curricular planning occurs in a consistent manner, since its main function will be developed based on the educational needs that arise in a given period, the ultimate goal is the fulfillment of the proposed objectives, taking into account that it is based on an interrelated set of constructs, approaches and criteria, constituted in a planned manner before the conduct of various actions with the characteristics that can be modified if necessary. Curricular planning has the particularity of orienting learning in order to guarantee better results for students, seen as a process of anticipating, carrying out and controlling activities that are involved in a phenomenon or context of an educational type, with the consequence of covering needs reflected in a diagnosis and therefore achieving the proposed goals within a given period of time.

The most elementary characteristics of the curriculum planning process in order for it to be efficient, according to Bolaños and Molina (1990), are the following

a) To be conceived as an integral process,
b) Be participatory.
c) To be seen as a permanent process.
d) Be flexible. (p. 110).

In this sense, we present the characteristics that curricular planning should possess, which should be done in a participatory manner as part of a teaching-learning process, integrating what is stipulated according to the national curriculum issued by the State and fulfilling the objectives established in phases in an organized and structured manner so that it adjusts to the various scenarios or contexts that may arise.

It should be noted that the importance of planning lies in the art of organizing coherently the achievements and objectives to be achieved from the educational point of view. Thus, decision-making is presented based on the requirements needed to address a given situation, to cover specific needs, taking into account national education policies as a legal basis, respecting the individuality of social actors. Planning is the starting point in many institutions and companies, since it allows for the design and organization of activities with previously set goals and objectives.

In relation to the above, it can also be mentioned that planning prioritizes the pedagogical task over administrative activities. Furthermore, its development, use and application are important because they are carried out based on its objectives, carrying out activities, making decisions and facilitating the achievement of goals by reducing risks.

However, this process has its phases which seek to describe and systematize the content, techniques and instruments to be taught in a given time, are classified as: diagnosis of the community, definition of educational objectives, determination of content, curriculum design, selection of methods and evaluation (See *Figure 3*).

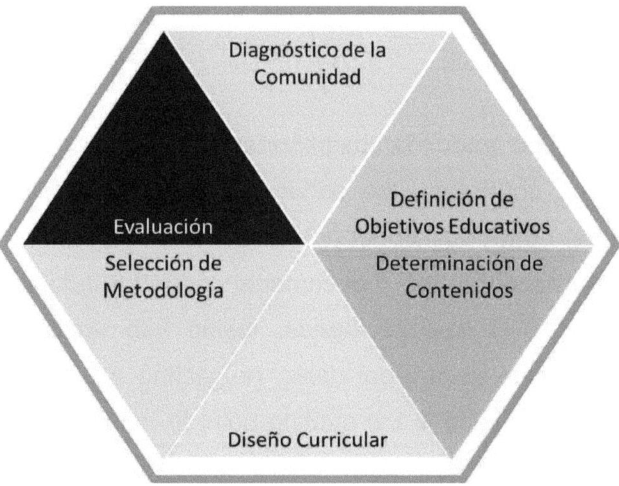

Figure 3. Phases of Curriculum Planning
Note: Source: Own elaboration. (2019).

Figure 3 shows the different phases that are addressed in curriculum planning, which can be read in a clockwise fashion as: Diagnosis of the community, established by Arango (1972), as: "the phase that will allow us to become aware of those problems for whose solution the professional will prepare" (p. 283). In this regard, this author emphasizes the function of training people to carry out specific actions for the resolution of problems. The second phase is the definition of educational objectives, related to the results that are expected to be obtained during the learning process. According to Arango (1972; 284), it can be defined as: "the description that the teacher makes in advance of the changes in behaviour that he expects to occur in the student as a consequence of learning". However, these may or may not be defined and will depend on the concatenation in the phases of curricular planning, since they are presented after the required diagnosis has been made.

Then, the third phase of content determination, for which it is necessary to have set the objectives, being these analyzed in depth to establish the knowledge, skills and attitudes to be acquired. The fourth phase, curricular design, determines the way in which the content will be transmitted according to its objective. Similarly, there is the fifth phase called methodology selection, which refers to existing methods, techniques and resources. Finally, there is the sixth phase of curriculum planning, which is an instrument that allows for the measurement of academic development according to each class plan.

METHOD

"All philosophical thought is based on experience.

Emmanuel Levinas.

The research method developed is the phenomenological-hermeneutical one, which already describes the world of life in order to understand it from the lived experience. In fact, the emphasis of this research method is on the interpretation of the meanings of the world and the actions of the subjects. These meanings emerge through dialogue and interactions, thus achieving an interpretation in social terms.

Methodological Approach

The approach addressed in this research refers to the qualitative one, known as Creswell (2007), as:

> a process of investigating the understanding of a social or human problem, based on the construction of a complex and holistic picture, formed by words, reporting with detailed views of the informants carried out in the natural environment. (p. 1)

According to what has been established, this research is focused on the study of social problems from their setting, where it will seek to investigate through reliable sources relevant information to interpret the results based on reality.

Type of Study

This study is framed in a field research, in this regard, Arias (2006), states that: "it consists of the collection of data directly from the subjects investigated, or from the reality where the events occur (primary data), without manipulating or controlling any variable" (p. 31). In the same vein, it is related to obtaining information that the researcher may have without altering the conditions in which he is found.

On the other hand, this research is considered to be of a descriptive type, meaning for Arias (2006): "the characterization of an event, phenomenon, individual or group, in order to establish its structure or behavior" (p. 24). In effect, it is the way in which the object of study is broken down in detail, and thus be able to identify the culture, behaviour or performance of a given population.

Research Scenario

The ideal scenario for research is one in which the observer obtains easy access, establishes a good immediate relationship with informants and collects data directly related to research interests. In this case the research was developed in a particular Educational Unit in Quito-Ecuador, which has all educational levels, from high school to unified general high school. It is relevant to mention that this institution works in the convergence of the Community-Education, due to the active participation of its members such as the family, students, teachers, administrative and support staff.

The Convergence of the Community-Education focuses on the common vision of education and the human-Christian style, helping the continuous formation in values, professional and Christian. This institution has provided its teaching staff with various types of training, most of which are related to its Educational Project and are even used as a basis for drawing up curricular plans; it has been shown that they adapt to the continuous changes in the guidelines in accordance with the timetables of the educational curriculum issued by the Ministry of Education of Ecuador, with reference to Ministerial Agreement No. 2016-00020-A of Ecuador.

Key Informant

The subgroup of key informants will be made up of 3 teachers, which are characterized as follows:

Subject 1: She is a School Religious Education Teacher who attends the 6th and 7th grades of General Basic Education. Her professionally obtained degree is a Bachelor of Education.

Subject 2: 6th grade teacher of Basic General Education who has the professional title of Lic.

Subject 3: Primary school teacher in the 3rd grade of General Basic Education. Her professional performance is for her career as a Pedagogical Science Teacher.

This is how the key informants in relation to the research are characterized, who through their participation allowed the elucidation of the existing reality in the study phenomenon.

Obtaining the Information

Data collection techniques are proposed by Rodríguez (2005) as: "the operational part of the investigative design, relates to the procedure, conditions and place of data collection" (p. 77). In this study, the main technique is the observation of the phenomenon, known as the visualization of the phenomenon and the context to be studied, a procedure that allows the discovery, evaluation and contrast of realities in the field of study.

Another technique used is the interview, which Tamayo and Tamayo (2004) propose as: "The direct relationship established between the researcher and his object of study through individuals or groups in order to obtain oral testimony" (p. 184). The type of interview used is the unstructured one characterized by its flexibility in the investigation process. In this study the validity was given through the triangulation of sources since it allowed the reinterpretation of the situation, in the light of the evidence from all the sources used in the investigation.

Information Analysis and Interpretation

To guarantee the systemic processing of the information, the methodological foundations of Leal (2005) were used, applying the technique of categorization by hermeneutic units to each of the interviews that were carried out. In accordance with the above, the information collected in the interviews was processed in a matrix called Epistemic Filter I, where the categories and properties emerged based on the verbalizations of the social actors. Then, a second matrix was used, called Epistemic Filter II, where the meanings and interpretation of the information were captured.

RESULTS

In order to respond to the inquiry and analysis of our object of study, we promoted the understanding of the reality in this case of curriculum evaluation and planning in the educational context from the discourse of the key informants of this research. In this sense, we present below a sample of the epistemic journey that allowed such interpretation based on informant 1 which was characterized by a pedagogical, young, enthusiastic and wise spirit. That is why with the affinity of the type of investigation developed and being located in the

Greek mythology he is identified as "Hebe", assistant of the gods. It should be noted that this process was carried out in the same way with Informant 2: Artemis characterized by being a serious and dedicated teacher; and Informant 3: Aphrodite characterized by having a deep love for education in values.

Epistemic Filter I

Informant 1: Hebe. Youth personification. Teacher with pedagogical spirit.

Epistemic Filter I. Informant 1: Hebe

Text	Concept	Properties	Categories
Inv: From the perspective of educational curriculum planning, what is the knowledge that you possess from your educational practice? Inf 1: Okay. Well I consider that the curricular planning is a formal process that every	Educational Processes in Curriculum Planning	-is a formal process that every educational institution must comply with.	Curriculum Planning

educational institution must comply with in order to comply with the educational management, in which the educational processes of teaching-learning are immersed. (...) Curricular planning is also the systematized and organized structure of all the content that must be given in a given time.		-to comply with educational management- -the teaching-learning educational processes. -in a certain amount of time. -systematized and organized structure of all the content	

Inv 2: How do you develop curriculum planning from your training area? Inf 1: Well mainly, before developing the planning I place myself in the academic grade I will attend. Then I place myself in the time I have to be able to develop it and I do the necessary documentary research according to the contents that I think need to be emphasized. The needs of the students depend on this, since I must make a diagnosis that allows me to analyze their weaknesses and strengths. (...) Once I have this diagnosis, I set contents, strategies and techniques.	Educational Process	-I place myself in the academic grade. -time I have to develop it. -documentary research needed according to the contents. -depends on the needs of the students.	Teaching-Learning Process

		-analyze weaknesses and strengths. -fixed contents, strategies and techniques.	
There are various evaluation techniques and instruments. Which of them do you use in	Evaluation techniques and instruments in the educational process.	-I like to work with group	Evaluation Techniques

curriculum planning to facilitate your pedagogical practice? Inf 1: Well, I like to work with group evaluation techniques, where students can learn to work as a team reflecting respect and solidarity among themselves. Let's see... I plan with exhibitions, workshops, work tables, and also individual ones, but in less quantity, like exams. Well and the instruments depend on the technique, it can be for the exam you use questionnaire questions and so on.		evaluation techniques. -learning to work as a team. -I plan with exhibitions, workshops, work tables. -the tests. -the test uses a questionnaire of questions.	and Instruments.

		-the instruments depend on the technique.	

Note: Informant 1 speech and categorization of the researcher (2019)

Interpretation of Hebe's emerging concepts.

In the discursive text presented in Epistemic Filter I of informant 1 Hebe, consulted through the interview technique on the evaluation and curriculum planning in the educational process, the following categories emerged:

In regard to the category "Curricular Planning", it is interpreted that the meaning that teachers attribute to planning is linked to the concept of "Educational Processes in Curricular Planning". In this sense, curricular planning is considered by Principals who Make School (2015) to be: "a teacher's tool, an unavoidable instance of reflection on what to teach and how to do it" (p. 1). Likewise, it allows teachers to reflect permanently and to anticipate, since it involves posing hypotheses regarding the teaching-learning process.

Another category that emerged from Hebe's discursive text was "Teaching-Learning Process", linked to the concept of "Educational Processes, known as the procedure by which special knowledge about a training area is transmitted, directly influencing the phenomenon of academic performance from the factors that determine its behavior. Finally, the category "Techniques and Instruments of Evaluation" emerged, being linked to the concept of "Techniques and Instruments of Evaluation in the Educational Process", being interpreted from the discourse of informant 1, it is known as the procedures used by the teacher to obtain information about the knowledge that students possess regarding a specific subject.

Epistemic Filter II

Informant 1: Hebe. Youth personification. Teacher with pedagogical spirit.

Epistemic Filter II. Informant 1.

Concept	Properties	Categories	Meaning	Interpretation
Educational Processes in Curriculum Planning	-is a formal process that every educational institution must comply with. -to comply with educational management- -the teaching-learning	Curriculum Planning	It is a process through which an educational reality is diagnosed in order to establish its problems, starting from its needs, and proposes objectives in an organized and systematized way to fulfill them within an educational framework.	All teachers within an educational institution must establish their reality in the study scenario through a diagnosis in order to develop the curriculum planning that determines the application of educational processes for quality management.

	educational processes. -in a certain amount of time. -systematized and organized structure of all the content			
Educational Process	-I place myself in the academic grade.	Teaching-Learning Process	It refers to the educational processes where content and the teacher must be taken	Emphasis needs to be placed on teaching-learning processes based on the needs, weaknesses, strengths and abilities of the

	-time I have to develop it. -documentary research needed according to the contents. -depends on the needs of the students. -analyze weaknesses and strengths.		into account in the teaching aspect, and educational experiences and the student in the learning aspect. These aspects are the fundamental bases of an effective and efficient educational process.	student in order to promote quality education.

	-fixed contents, strategies and techniques.			
Evaluation techniques and instruments in	-I like to work with group evaluation techniques.	Evaluation Techniques and Instruments.	The techniques and instruments of evaluation are indispensable tools in	It is necessary to know that the techniques are different from the instruments, in addition each evaluation technique has characteristics that determine the types of

the educational process.	-learning to work as a team. -I plan with exhibitions, workshops, work tables. -the tests. -the test uses a questionnaire of questions. -the instruments depend on the technique.		the educational process that allow to know the performance of the students in the areas of formation and others.	instruments that can be used to collect the information needed.

Note: Source: Own elaboration. (2019).

Before starting the triangulation process, a reduction of data was made mainly at the physical level, while the second is presented at the conceptual level. The reduction is based on the ability to order, categorize, prioritize and interrelate the data according to emerging patterns of interpretation. From there, the emerging categories are integrated into the discursive texts in Macrocategories, in order to change the nature of the categories from coded facts to constructs for a better hermeneutic interpretation in the triangulation process. The following are the Macrocategories that emerged from the discourse of the three (03) informants:

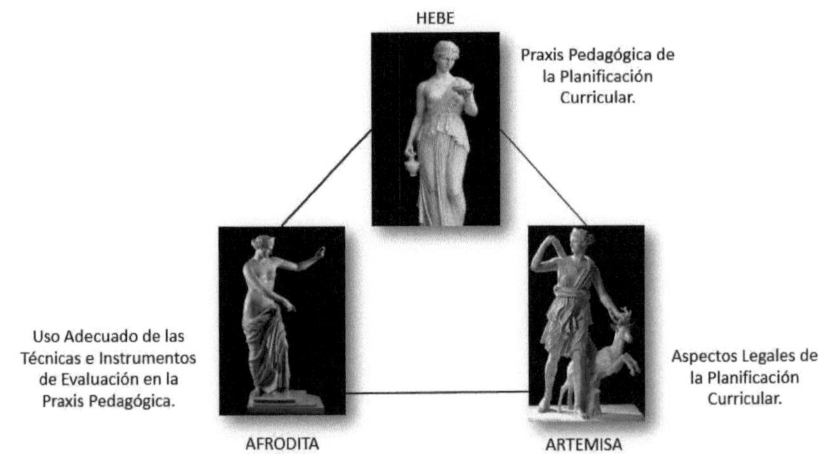

Figure 4. Representation of the emerging macro-categories.

Triangulation Process

Below is a sample of the contrast-triangulation process based on Informant 1: Hebe. It should be noted that this process was carried out in the same way with Informant 2: Artemis and Informant 3: Aphrodite.

Macrocategory 1. Pedagogical Praxis of Curriculum Planning

Informant (Hebe)	Theoretical Confrontation	Researcher's position
... the educational processes of teaching-learning, ... in a certain time, ... systematized and organized structure of all the content, ... I place myself in the academic grade, ... analyze the weaknesses and strengths.	According to Meléndez and Gómez (2008), curricular planning in pedagogical practice should be: "a reflection in the light of the constructivist paradigm, from the to group programmatic content with values up to the construction	Curricular planning is a process of building activities that promote cognitive skills in the student through the use of tools that ensure the fulfillment of objectives to be

	of pedagogical and didactic environments that make experiences possible" (p. 371). The teaching practice is in line with the pedagogy given by the teacher to his or her students; it is closely related to curricular planning since it is the basic structure for fulfilling the educational processes.	taught in educational practice.

Note: The researcher based on the information collected (2019).

Macrocategory 2. Legal Aspects in Curricular Planning.

Informant (Hebe)	Theoretical Confrontation	Researcher's position
is a formal process that every educational institution must comply with. to fulfill the educational management,... time I have to be able to develop it.	Curricular planning in Ecuador is based on the guidelines issued by the Ministry of Education of Ecuador in its Ministerial Agreement Nº 2016-00020-A in order to achieve the educational objectives corresponding to each area, as well as on the country's educational quality standards.	Each curriculum planning process must be covered by the legal guidelines of the country's educational entity. This institutional body is the one that dictates the parameters to follow in order to comply with the educational process.

Note: Source: Researcher based on information collected (2019).

Macrocategory 3. Appropriate use of Evaluation Techniques and Instruments in Pedagogical Praxis

Informant (Hebe)	Theoretical Confrontation	Researcher's position
...documentary research necessary according to the contents,... depending on the needs of the students,... fixed contents, strategies and techniques.	Assessment techniques and instruments are set and used to collect, analyse and judge on the evidence the student brings to their learning. This evidence may be knowledge, process or product evidence.	Every teacher should know the difference between evaluation techniques and the instruments to be used for each of them. Well, these tools are those that will allow him/her to apply and evaluate how the educational process develops in the students.

Note: The researcher based on the information collected (2019)

CONCLUDING THOUGHTS

In the journey through the hermeneusis made to the concepts, properties and categories emerging from the discursive text of the informants in this qualitative research, important considerations arise that give response to the investigative purposes that propitiated it. With respect to the knowledge of curriculum planning in the teachers of the Educational Unit located in Quito, Ecuador, it can be emphasized that the teachers have a notion of what it means, recognizing it as the tool or systematized structure that will allow them to organize the contents to be dealt with in the educational process.

On the other hand, it should be mentioned that the curriculum planning process carried out by these teachers is based above all on compliance with the content to be developed, justified by the development of the skills and abilities of the students, rather than by time loads. Likewise, it was possible to learn that the assessment techniques that are most used are work tables, presentations and exams to encourage students to work in teams; however, there are others that, through their instruments, can help make pedagogical practice more dynamic.

BIBLIOGRAPHY

Arango, J. (1972). Curriculum planning and evaluation according to a country's needs. *Medical Education and Health.* [Article online] Pan American Health Organization PAHO. Retrieved from: http://cort.as/-Hs5v [Accessed: May 2019]

Arias, F. (2006). *The research project. Introduction to scientific methodology.* (5th ed.). Caracas: Editorial Episteme

Bolaños, G and Molina, Z. (1990). *Introduction to the Curriculum.* Costa Rica: EUNED

Creswell, J. (2007). *Qualitative inquiry and research design: Choosing among five approaches (2ª ed.).* Thousand Oaks, CA, US: Sage Publications, Inc

Principals Who Go to School (2015). *Advice on Curriculum Planning.* Buenos Aires: OEI

National Institute for Educational Evaluation INEVAL (2018). *Organic Statute of Organizational Management by Processes of the National Institute for Educational Evaluation.* Ecuador. Retrieved from: http://cort.as/-R5Nt

Leal, J. (2005). *The autonomy of the research subject and research methodology.* University of the Andes. Venezuela: Centro Editorial Litorama.

Meléndez, M and Gómez (2008). Curriculum planning in the classroom. Un modelo de enseñanza por competencias. *Revista de Educación LAURUS, 14*(26) 367-392. Retrieved from: https://www.redalyc.org/pdf/761/76111491018.pdf

MINEDU (2016). *National Basic Education Curriculum.* Approved by Ministerial Resolution - 281-2016-Minedu. Ecuador.

MINEDU (2017). *Instructions for curricular planning for the national education system.* Ecuador.

Navarro, N; Falconí, A and Espinoza, J. (2017). Improving the evaluation process of students in basic education. *University and Society 9*(4). Retrieved from: http://cort.as/-R4jY

Rodríguez, E. (2005) *Metodología de la Investigación. Creativity, rigor and integrity are factors that transform the student into a successful professional.* Mexico: Universidad Juarez Autonoma de Tabasco. Academic Division of Engineering and Architecture

Rosales, C. (1990). To *evaluate is to reflect on teaching.* (3rd ed.). Madrid: Narcea

Strauss, A. and Corbin, J. (2002). *Bases de la investigación cualitativa. Techniques and procedures for developing Grounded Theory.* Medellín: University of Antioquia

Tamayo, M. (2004). *The Process of Scientific Research.* Editorial Limusa.

Vázquez, L. (2011). *Incidence of the evaluation instruments in the development of the metacognitive competences of the first year students of the Pedagogy, Psychology and Education Faculty of the Catholic University of Cuenca in the third quarter of the 2009-2010 academic year*. [Undergraduate work to apply for the degree of Master in Teaching and Curriculum for Higher Education] Universidad Técnica de Ambato. Ecuador. Retrieved from: http://cort.as/-QzHe

Printed by Books on Demand GmbH, Norderstedt / Germany